OUTDOOR ADVENTURE!
HUNTING

Adam G. Klein

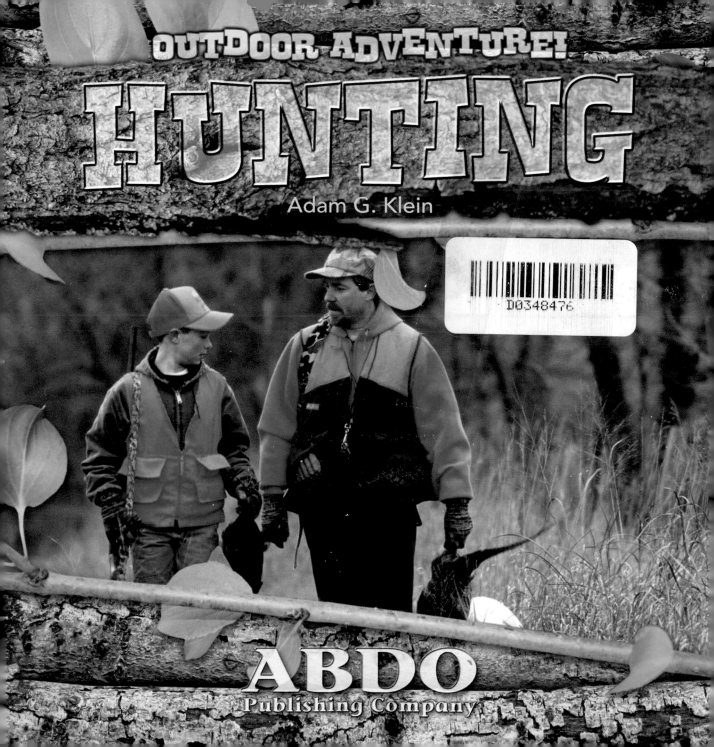

ABDO
Publishing Company

visit us at
www.abdopublishing.com

Published by ABDO Publishing Company, 8000 West 78th Street, Edina, Minnesota 55439.
Copyright © 2008 by Abdo Consulting Group, Inc. International copyrights reserved in all
countries. No part of this book may be reproduced in any form without written permission from the
publisher. The Checkerboard Library™ is a trademark and logo of ABDO Publishing Company.

Printed in the United States.

Cover Photo: Corbis
Interior Photos: AP Images pp. 11, 20, 21, 22, 26; Comstock p. 17; Corbis pp. 1, 18, 23, 24, 29;
     Corel Stock Photo Library pp. 5, 7, 19; iStockphoto pp. 9, 11, 13, 14, 15; Neil Klinepier p. 16;
     Peter Arnold pp. 6, 27

Series Coordinator: Rochelle Baltzer
Editors: Rochelle Baltzer, Megan M. Gunderson
Art Direction & Cover Design: Neil Klinepier

Library of Congress Cataloging-in-Publication Data

Klein, Adam G., 1976-
  Hunting / Adam G. Klein.
      p. cm. -- (Outdoor adventure!)
  Includes index.
  ISBN 978-1-59928-960-1
  1. Hunting--Juvenile literature. I. Title.

  SK35.5.K54 2008
  799.2--dc22
                                        2007029168

CONTENTS

HUNTING TALES

The silence was heavy while Hank and Jenny crouched next to the cold pond. Jenny's hunting dog, Buddy, sat quietly on alert for a flock of birds. The only sound was the damp morning breeze rustling the tall reeds.

Suddenly, Jenny, Hank, and Buddy were no longer alone. "Do you see we're surrounded by ducks?" Jenny whispered to Hank. Hank realized what she meant. He had never seen so many ducks before!

Just then, Buddy burst out of the reeds to chase something. His movement sent the startled ducks flying into the air. They circled the pond a few times before shrinking into distant specks in the sky.

Hank and Jenny did not get a single shot that morning. And, they did not spot any more ducks the entire day. Still, being in the middle of the **chaotic** (kay-AH-tihk) duck scramble became one of their favorite hunting stories.

Ducks are considered either puddle ducks or diving ducks. Puddle ducks, such as the mallard, live in shallow marshes and rivers. Diving ducks, such as the canvasback, dwell in large lakes and rivers.

WHY HUNT?

Every year, millions of hunters tread into fields and woods in search of **game**. Venturing into the wilderness is good for your health. Exercise keeps your body strong, and fresh air relieves **stress**. People hunt for many reasons. Over the years, these motives have changed.

Originally, gathering food was the main reason to hunt. There was no other way for people in early civilizations

Some hunters collect trophies and mount them on walls.

CAN YOU IDENTIFY BEAR TRACKS?

to obtain meat. Today, some people still find satisfaction in hunting their own food instead of purchasing it at grocery stores.

Finding **trophies** motivates other hunters. These people might collect antlers or furs from certain animals. Perfecting shooting skills is another reason for people to venture into the wilderness.

A small but growing group of people are nature hunters. They feel that hunting brings them closer to nature. For them, hunting is about humans taking an active part in the natural world.

Hunting is challenging. It takes much practice to develop the skills necessary for shooting **game**. Many people hunt more than one type of animal, too. In this case, they must learn about each animal before **embarking** on their hunt.

WHAT TO HUNT

When planning a hunting trip, hunters must first decide what animals they want to take. They can hunt birds, such as ducks, pheasant, quail, or partridge. Or they can take larger creatures, such as deer, moose, or elk. Hunters occasionally get a chance to track rabbit or squirrels. Certain places offer a hunting season for bears, too.

Worldwide hunting provides other challenges. On African **safaris**, hunters track **exotic** animals such as leopards or elephants. In Australia, some hunters seek kangaroos. Certain animals can be difficult to find. Yet, many hunters enjoy the challenge.

Other hunters have different goals in mind. They may wish to hunt a particular animal from every continent. Or, they may want **trophies** to display. A trophy hunter's goal might be to obtain the biggest rack of deer antlers he or she can find.

FOLLOW A RABBIT'S TRAIL!

TIP *Tell someone where you plan to hunt and when you expect to return. That way, he or she can more easily help you if needed.*

Since the mid–1900s, game-management organizations have restored the white-tailed deer population to abundance in the United States.

LOCATIONS

After hunters have determined what animal they wish to hunt, they must find a place to get it. States provide public land for hunting. Usually, people must pay a fee to hunt on the land. They must also have a local hunting license.

In addition, state laws limit when hunting is allowed. And, they determine the number of animals a hunter may take. Hunters must obey these rules to avoid a fine.

People can hunt on private land as well. But, they must obtain permission from the owner in advance. They should offer information about themselves, including their hunting license numbers. And if they want to return, they must respect the owner's property.

Private preserves are another type of hunting location. Individuals or groups may own private preserves. Most preserves are operated by membership. Members pay a fee to hunt on this land.

Some hunters see their sport as a contest between the hunter and the hunted. Though hunters use weapons, animals have several advantages. They move faster, are more familiar with their surroundings, and can smell and hear better.

Owners of private preserves control the types and the number of animals available for hunting. Some owners make the surroundings resemble a particular hunting location, such as a southern plantation or a duck marsh. Many private preserves also offer dog training, **accommodations**, and shooting sport activities.

METHODS

There are many different hunting methods. Stalking is one way hunters track **game**. Following an animal's trail can lead you to the animal itself.

Pheasant and quail hunters walk through fields in a line. They use hunting dogs to locate and flush out game within gun range. Each hunter has a specific shooting zone. As the hunters move, the birds flee. Then, each hunter takes a turn shooting at birds in his or her zone.

People often hunt deer from elevated platforms called deer stands. Deer stands are built in areas with many signs of animal activity. They provide a place for hunters to wait for deer without being seen.

Other times, hunters must find ways to attract animals. **Mimicking** a turkey's call is likely to draw in a wild turkey. Animals such as deer are attracted to scents. And, duck or geese hunters often place

CAN YOU TRACK A PHEASANT?

groups of decoys in water. Then, the real birds fly in to see what the pretend birds find so interesting!

Puddle ducks rest in looser groups than diving ducks. So, some hunters leave as much as ten feet (3 m) between each decoy.

HUNTING DOGS

Occasionally, hunters require help from an expert. That's when dogs are needed. Dogs have a strong sense of smell, which makes them excellent hunting aids. Hunters use dogs to flush or track animals.

Retrieving breeds, such as the Labrador retriever, are well suited for bringing in waterfowl. This is because their skin produces an oily substance that sheds water.

Certain dog **breeds** point at animals. When a pointing dog has located an animal, it stands in a rigid position. This lets the hunter know where to shoot. Other breeds **retrieve** animals after they have been shot.

Before **embarking** on a hunt, a dog must be thoroughly trained. To train a dog, its owner exposes it to the scents it will seek during a hunt. The dog should also become familiar with hunting conditions, including the sound of a gunshot. Most important, a hunting dog must obey its owner's commands.

Dogs are not always allowed to accompany hunters. For example, some states do not allow bear hunters to use dogs. Some people believe this method is **unethical**. Others worry about dogs **trespassing** on private property. So, hunters must be sure to check the rules for the areas they plan to hunt in!

HUNTING TOOLS

Hunters often find themselves in cold, wet, or muddy places. Therefore, they should prepare for difficult conditions. A good pair of boots helps a hunter cross difficult **terrain**. And, warm socks and layers of clothing protect a hunter from harsh weather conditions.

Another hunting necessity is a knife. Hunters use knives for many tasks, including cleaning **game**. Knives should be less than four inches (10 cm) long. And, they should be made from strong materials, such as carbon and stainless steel. Still, knives eventually become dull or break. So, bringing a spare is a good idea.

Other hunting items are important for survival. To survive outdoors,

LOOK FOR MOOSE PRINTS!

To clean game, a hunter uses a knife to cut out the parts of an animal that are unfit for food.

hunters must know their **bearings**. Maps, compasses, and Global Positioning System (GPS) receivers help hunters avoid getting lost. And, binoculars help them locate landmarks, **game**, and even other hunters. In addition, hunters should always bring a first aid kit, high-calorie snacks, and water.

GPS determines precise times and positions. With receivers, it allows people to find their locations anywhere on the earth.

FIREARMS

Of all the tools for a hunt, a gun is usually the most important. There are a variety of firearms to choose from. The most common types used for hunting are shotguns and rifles.

Shotguns have a short range. They spray tiny round pellets toward a target in a **diverging** pattern. Therefore, hunters can hit moving targets more easily than by firing one bullet from a rifle.

Hunters should practice using a gun before going on a hunt.

Shotguns are used for fast small **game**, including birds and rabbit. However, shotguns can still be used to shoot larger game, such as deer. In this case, a hunter would load a shotgun with one large round bullet called a slug.

Hunters use rifles when shooting moose, elk, or other large creatures. Rifles have a much longer range than shotguns. They are also more **accurate**. The accuracy comes from grooves that spiral down the rifle barrel's interior. These grooves make the bullet spin. Similar to a spiraling football, this spin makes the bullet more stable.

EARLY ARMS

Some hunters prefer to experience the way people hunted long ago. So they use traditional weapons, such as **muzzle**-loaders and bows and arrows.

Today's muzzle-loaders are designed to model original firearms, which are hundreds of years old. To load a muzzle-loader, **black powder** is poured into the barrel. Then, a barrier called a patch is placed on the muzzle.

Muzzle-loading rifles are used for hunting small game and varmints.

Finally, **ammunition** is added. The type of ammunition depends on the size of the animal a hunter seeks.

Muzzle-loaders have some disadvantages. They are not weatherproof, and they offer only one shot before reloading is required. Still, many people enjoy the challenge.

The bow and arrow has been used by hunters for thousands of years. This weapon is ideal for shooting large **game**, such as deer.

Bow and arrow hunting requires much skill and strength. Hunters must get close enough to an animal for a good shot. A bow's draw weight determines how strong the archer must be. For example, a 40-pound (18-kg) bow requires 40 pounds of force to draw an arrow.

Bow hunting is popular for many reasons. Bow hunters are generally allowed longer hunting seasons. Plus, the challenge of hunting with a bow makes the sport more rewarding for many people.

STAY SAFE

Using a weapon is a major responsibility. Most hunting accidents occur because hunters do not know what they are shooting at. If you are not completely aware of your target or what is near it, do not fire! This rule holds true when using any kind of weapon.

In some situations, hunters do not wear orange. That way, they can stay hidden from animals.

Wearing orange is a bright reminder to be safe. Orange makes a hunter more visible to other hunters. Most color-blind people can still detect bright orange. Yet, most large **game** see only black, white, and shades of gray. So, orange clothing will alert people and not animals.

Some state laws require hunters to take a class before obtaining a license. Taking a hunting class is beneficial even if it is not necessary for you. Classes provide information about regulations, weapon safety, and hunting methods. Other hunters in your group will appreciate and respect your knowledge of the sport, too.

TIP *Never wave to make another hunter aware of you. This could attract fire. Instead, yell in a loud voice and stay hidden.*

The two-handed, or "ready," gun carry offers the best control in thick brush and when hunters must fire quickly.

GUN SAFETY

Since 1871, the National Rifle Association of America (NRA) has governed the sport of shooting with rifles and pistols. In civilian training, the NRA continues to be the leader in firearms education. The NRA has several fundamental rules for safe gun handling.

1. **Always keep the gun pointed in a safe direction.**
2. **Always keep your finger off the trigger until ready to shoot.**
3. **Always keep the gun unloaded until ready to use.**

In addition, follow these safety tips when hunting with a gun.

- *Know your target and what is beyond it. Never fire at only sound or movement or in a direction where there might be other people.*
- *Hold your gun at all times. Leaning it against a tree or any other object is very dangerous.*
- *Wear ear protectors and shooting glasses. Guns make loud noises and may release damaging debris or hot gas.*

IN THE PAST

For many people, hunting is a long-standing tradition. Its history traces back thousands of years. Today, the sport generally involves finding animals and showing skill. But this philosophy was not always practiced in an **ethical** way.

In the United States during the 1800s, unregulated hunting turned into regular killing. Hunters killed thousands of animals at once. They sold many of them at market. Sadly, just as many were left to waste.

Market hunters used many methods to kill ducks. They worked from before dawn until dusk to take as many ducks as possible.

Something had to be done to protect the American wilderness from destruction. So in 1887, Theodore Roosevelt and several friends founded the Boone and Crockett Club. The club set up guidelines for **ethical** hunting. These standards, which are still used, protect the **environment**.

Unfortunately, market hunting had already caused many animal populations to **decline** severely. In the early 1900s, bison and wild turkeys nearly became extinct. It was already too late to save some species. Passenger pigeons had once made up a large part of eastern and central North America's bird population. Sadly, they became extinct in 1914.

FAIR CHASE

Fair chase involves hunting in a way that does not give hunters an unfair advantage over wild animals. To promote fair chase, the Boone and Crockett Club established a list of ethics related to hunting.

1. Obey all laws and regulations.
2. Respect the customs of the area where the hunting occurs.
3. Behave in a way that positively reflects your hunting abilities and sensibilities.
4. Attain and maintain the skills necessary to make the kill as certain and quick as possible.
5. Behave in a way that will not bring dishonor to the hunter, the hunted, or the environment.
6. Recognize that these principles are intended to improve the hunter's experience of the relationship between predator and prey. This relationship is one of the most fundamental relationships of humans and their environment.

CONSERVATION

Today, the greatest threat to animal species is loss of **environment**. To survive, animals need places to find food and shelter. Therefore, organizations work hard to preserve land for animals.

To pay for environmental issues, the federal government introduced duck stamps in 1934. These stamps have brought in more than $670 million, which has been used to preserve natural **habitats**. Duck stamps have restored more than 5 million acres (2 million ha) of land!

Ninety-eight cents from every dollar generated by federal duck stamp sales goes directly toward protecting wetland habitats.

Other conservation programs have also been successful. For example, turkey populations are stronger than ever. This is because wildlife restoration programs moved wild

Wild turkeys can run at speeds of up to 25 miles per hour (40 km/h) and fly up to 55 miles per hour (89 km/h)!

turkeys from places where they were most common to areas with few or no turkeys. They made sure these places had resources for the relocated turkeys to survive. In the 1900s, there were about 30,000 turkeys in the United States. Today, there are more than 7 million turkeys!

FAIR HUNTING

Despite efforts to protect wildlife, some hunters practice poaching. Poaching is not sportsmanship. It includes hunting without a license, taking above the legal limit, and using unfair hunting methods. Using poison arrows or blinding deer with bright lights at night is **unethical**.

Hunting laws were made to prevent such instances. Some laws regulate the amount of animals taken. Others require that animals be taken fairly. The penalty for poaching can include a fine of thousands of dollars and time in jail.

A common excuse for poachers is "because I can." This is true. People can do whatever they want. Of course, the better choice is "I can do what is right." Poachers bring a bad name to hunting. They ruin the good reputation of the millions of hunters that respect their sport.

By following the rules, you can enjoy the hunting experience. With proper **stewardship**, there will be plenty of animals to take. It won't be long before you will walk away with amazing stories, just like Hank and Jenny did. So, get out there and have fun on your own hunting adventure!

Hunting can be a fun activity to share with family and friends. In fact, about 16 million people purchase hunting licenses in the United States each year!

GLOSSARY

accommodation - something supplied for convenience or to satisfy a need. Accommodations can include lodging, food, or other services.

accurate - free of errors.

ammunition - bullets, shells, and other items used in firearms.

bearings - the comprehension of one's position, environment, or situation.

black powder - an explosive mixture used especially in fireworks and as a propellant in old-fashioned firearms.

breed - a group of animals sharing the same appearance and characteristics.

chaotic - of or relating to a state of total confusion.

decline - to tend toward an inferior state or a weaker condition.

diverging - extending in different directions from a common point.

embark - to make a start.

environment - all the surroundings that affect the growth and well-being of a living thing.

ethical - morally right. Something unethical is morally wrong.

exotic - interesting because it is strange or different from the usual.

game - wild animals hunted for food or sport.

habitat - a place where a living thing Is naturally found.

mimic - to imitate or copy.

muzzle - the discharging end of a weapon.

retrieve - to locate and bring in.

safari - a journey or a hunting trip in Africa.

stewardship - the careful and responsible management of something entrusted to one's care.

stress - a physical, chemical, or emotional factor that causes bodily or mental unrest and may be involved in causing some diseases.

terrain - the physical features of an area of land. Mountains, rivers, and canyons can all be part of a terrain.

trespass - to unlawfully enter another person's property.

trophy - a game animal or fish suitable for mounting.

WEB SITES

To learn more about hunting, visit ABDO Publishing Company on the World Wide Web at **www.abdopublishing.com**. Web sites about hunting are featured on our Book Links page. These links are routinely monitored and updated to provide the most current information available.

INDEX